BOREDOMISM

THE ART OF STILLNESS AND PRESENCE

MOHD IYAAD DILNAWAZ MUKADAM

Made with ♥ on the Notion Press Platform
www.notionpress.com

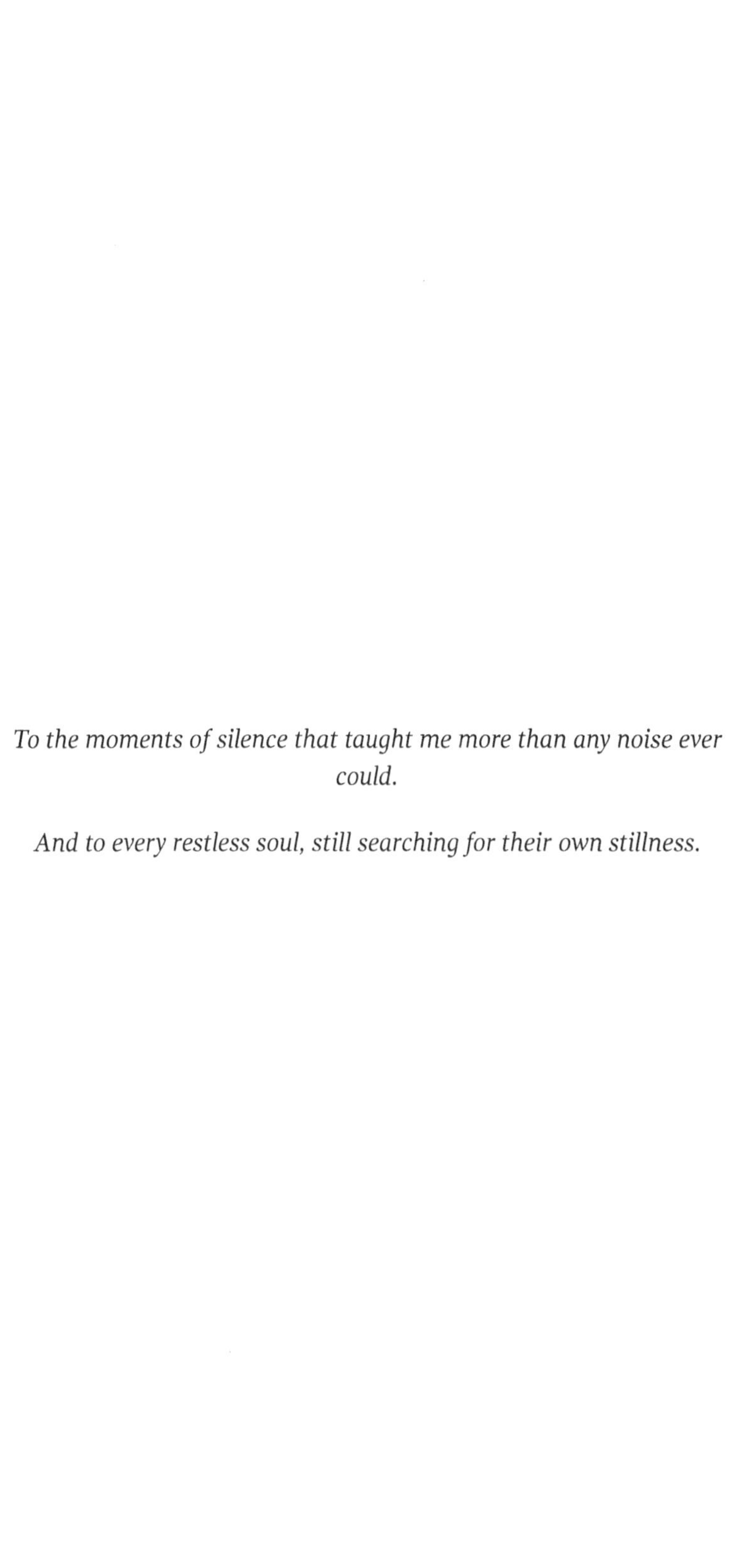

To the moments of silence that taught me more than any noise ever could.

And to every restless soul, still searching for their own stillness.

Contents

Contents

Preface

This book was not planned in a rush, nor written in the heat of inspiration. It was shaped slowly, like stone softened by water.
It began with a single question that haunted my quiet moments: What if doing nothing is not a failure, but a forgotten art?

We live in an age where busyness is a virtue, and boredom is seen as a flaw. We measure our days by tasks completed, our worth by the noise we make. I did too—until stillness found me, not as an enemy, but as a teacher.

Boredomism is not a philosophy of abandonment. It is a philosophy of return—to simplicity, to presence, to the quiet places within us we have long ignored.
Writing this book was an act of slowing down, of listening, of honoring the spaces between thoughts.

I do not offer answers here. I offer invitations— to pause, to notice, to exist without apology. If you find even a fragment of yourself mirrored in these pages, then this book has done what it was meant to do.

Acknowledgements

This book could not have been written without the silent encouragement of those who allowed me space to be still.

To my family and friends—thank you for understanding my need for quiet, for never rushing me when I needed slowness, and for believing in the value of this work even before it had a name.

To the thinkers, writers, and philosophers whose ideas shaped the edges of my own—your echoes are everywhere, even where they are invisible.

And to every moment of boredom that I once feared, but later welcomed—you were never a void. You were always a doorway. Thank you.

Prologue

This book begins as many different questions. I noticed how uncomfortable we've grown with pause, space, and slowness. We check our phones in elevators, queues, even during conversations. We feel anxious in the absence of input. As if being alone with our thoughts is a problem to solve.

This book is my attempt to slow that down. Not to offer solutions or tips, but to propose a shift—a new mental posture toward boredom.

Boredomism is not a technique. It is a re-framing. It invites a return to intentional emptiness, not as a void, but as a resource.

This book was not born from a desire to impress, to inform for the sake of knowledge, or to offer yet another framework for becoming something else. It was born from stillness. From a long pause in which the usual noises of ambition, productivity, and progress faded into the background, and something quieter—yet far more honest—emerged.

We live in a time where we are taught to be afraid of boredom, as if it signals failure. The moment silence stretches too long, we reach for distractions. We fill every gap in our day with noise—content, conversations, scrolling, or planning. But beneath that endless motion lies an untended field. Boredom is not emptiness. It is space. It is possibility. And more importantly, it is a mirror. This book exists to hold up that mirror.

The world is speeding up, and with it, our nervous systems, our expectations, and our sense of time. We are constantly becoming—but rarely being. There is little room left to breathe, to notice, or to just exist without the need to justify our existence. That's why this book had to be written—not to add more noise, but to encourage the daring act of quieting down.

Boredomism emerged not as an ideology or a philosophy to follow like a rulebook, but as an exploration—one that many of us have already begun unknowingly in the pauses of life we often resist. This book gives those pauses a language, a structure, and an understanding. It proposes that perhaps doing nothing isn't nothing at all. Perhaps it's a sacred act of rebellion, of realignment, of remembering.

This book exists for the overwhelmed and the overachieving, for the restless and the burned out, for the thinkers who no longer want to think so much, and for the feelers who haven't felt anything real in a long time. It exists to say what has been quietly waiting to be said: that you do not need to constantly prove your worth. That your stillness is not your weakness, but your return.

If you've found your way here, maybe you already know that something in the current rhythm isn't working. Maybe you're seeking an unnamed peace. This book does not promise answers—but it offers an invitation: to be still long enough to hear the ones already whispering within you.

Introduction

In a world that rewards speed, noise, and endless activity, boredom has been cast aside—misunderstood as laziness or a lack of meaning. But what if boredom, in its quiet discomfort, is not a curse to avoid but a doorway to something deeper? What if doing nothing could reveal everything?

This part of the book gently guides you into the heart of that idea. It sets the stage for what follows, not with rules or complex theories, but with curiosity, openness, and a challenge to pause. You won't find urgency here—you'll find space. Space to reflect, to feel, and to consider the possibility that stillness holds more wisdom than we've been led to believe.

These early chapters are an invitation. To let go of the rush. To rethink what matters. And to step into the soft, often uncomfortable, but deeply honest terrain of doing nothing—on purpose.

Welcome to Boredomism.

CHAPTER ONE

WHAT IS BOREDOMISM?

Boredomism is a philosophical lens that reinterprets boredom—not as a negative state to escape, but as an essential part of being human that we've forgotten how to sit with.

It is the art of doing nothing—on purpose. Not for productivity. Not for relaxation. Not for any external reward. But simply to exist, observe, and be.

This philosophy doesn't glorify laziness. It doesn't reject ambition.

It simply questions a world where constant stimulation has become a survival mechanism.

We are not overworked. We are just overstimulated in such a way that makes our brain think that boredom is an ill and it must be cured.

Boredomism is created on the questions:

- Why we get bored?
- Why do we assume boredom as an ill?
- What happens when we stop trying to fill every second?
- What might we find in the emptiness we have learned so far?

CHAPTER TWO

WHY IS BOREDOM THE NEED OF HOUR?

In a world that's always in motion, boredom seems like a flaw—something to avoid, suppress, or escape. But what if it isn't a failure of stimulation... but a signal? What if boredom is the quiet knock at the door that reminds us we've wandered too far from ourselves?

Boredomism repositions boredom as not just a natural part of the human condition, but as a necessary one. Below are the core reasons boredom holds meaning in our overstimulated lives:

1. **We've Declared War on Emptiness**

    Modern society has developed an intolerance toward any space that feels empty or unproductive. From social media feeds that refresh endlessly, to entertainment platforms that never stop suggesting, the world has been engineered to avoid stillness at all costs. It's not just that we want distraction—it's that we've come to need it, even crave it, in moments that used to belong to silence.

    This constant engagement isn't neutral. It trains our brains to expect stimulation and equates movement with meaning. As a result, we lose our ability to sit in moments that feel "uneventful." But boredom, in its quiet discomfort, is often the only way the deeper parts of our mind come forward. When we eliminate the space for it, we lose access to clarity, introspection, and the emotional residue that never got processed.

2. **We Fear what we might Feel**

More than distraction, we've developed a fear of what boredom might reveal. In the moments when the world goes quiet, so do our defenses. The unresolved thoughts begin to rise. The existential weight we buried in activity begins to surface. And we panic—not because we don't know what to do, but because we're finally forced to confront what we've been avoiding.

This is the psychological cost of overstimulation. The fear of boredom is often the fear of self. But Boredomism teaches that this confrontation isn't something to fear—it's something to understand. Only by sitting through it can we learn how much of our behavior is just escape in disguise.

3. **We've Redefined "Doing Nothing" as a Failure**

In today's culture, rest has become a performance. Even self-care is marketed as a form of optimization. Doing nothing for its own sake feels almost immoral. We're praised for hustle, for productivity, for always having something going on. But that expectation is a trap. It detaches us from rhythms that once came naturally—slowness, reflection, seasonal energy, inward time.

To "do nothing" now requires conscious effort. It feels countercultural, even rebellious. Boredomism offers a different definition: doing nothing is not inactivity, but intentional unproductivity. A necessary space for the soul to breathe without the burden of output

4. **Attention has been Monetized**

Attention has become a commodity—bought, sold, and extracted like oil. We're not just distracted; we are constantly being targeted for distraction. Every scroll, every tap, every alert pulls our focus outward, leaving less space for inward presence. The more we outsource our attention, the more foreign our own minds begin to feel.

Boredomism challenges this. It reclaims attention not as a tool, but as a sacred currency. It suggests that to be bored—and stay bored—is a form of resistance. A way of telling the world, "You don't get to own my mind."

5. **Purpose has become a Performance**

We've been conditioned to believe that every moment must carry visible purpose. Whether through productivity, progress, or social proof, even our rest must be justified. A walk isn't just a walk—it's mindfulness. A break isn't just a break—it's "resetting my performance levels." In this system, silence is inefficiency. Slowness is weakness.

But not every moment needs to move you forward. Boredomism proposes that some moments should go nowhere. Purpose doesn't always have to look like effort. Sometimes the truest value is in not needing a reason.

6. **Stillness Feels Foreign-because we are Addicted to Movement**

We say we're tired, but we rarely rest. We stop working, but we never stop consuming. The nervous system never gets to fully deactivate. So when we do finally sit in stillness, it feels strange—even wrong. That discomfort is not boredom. It's withdrawal. The echo of too much motion.

Boredomism doesn't promise instant peace. It simply allows us to feel the effects of too much doing and begin to recover. Stillness isn't easy, but it's necessary. And the discomfort is the signal that healing has begun.

7. **Mental Fatigue and the Hijacked Nervous System**

We often think we're just "tired," but the truth is deeper: we're mentally overloaded, and our nervous systems are stuck in survival mode. Constant notifications, micro-decisions, background noise, and the pressure to stay "available" are wearing us down. It's not physical exhaustion—it's neural overstimulation. We're running on adrenaline, not intention.

Boredom, in this context, is not a weakness to avoid—it's the body's request for recalibration. It's how your system whispers, "I need quiet. I need time." Boredomism encourages this restoration. By stepping back from hyperactivity, we allow the nervous system to return to a more balanced state—one not ruled by urgency, but by awareness. It's not laziness—it's nervous system hygiene.

CHAPTER THREE

WHO IS THIS PHILOSOPHY FOR?

This philosophy is not for those seeking shortcuts or high-speed answers. It is not for those who wish to escape life but rather for those who wish to return to it in its most unfiltered form. Boredomism is for the thinkers who are tired of thinking, the doers who are tired of doing, and the wanderers who have grown weary of chasing destinations that disappear upon arrival.

It is for the over-stimulated mind and the under-nourished soul. For those who have filled their schedules, scrolled endlessly, and still felt a deep emptiness at the core of all that activity. This is for the person who feels like they're constantly becoming—but can't remember the last time they simply were. For anyone who's ever asked themselves in a quiet moment, "Is this all there is?" and meant it not cynically, but curiously.

Boredomism is for artists and professionals, students and retirees, introverts and extroverts alike. It speaks to anyone caught in the current of modern speed, yearning to slow down but unsure how. It is for the ones who don't just want more time—they want more meaning in the time they already have. It is especially for those who feel guilty when they rest, and who are searching for a permission they never knew they needed.

If you're here, if you're holding this book and reading these words, then perhaps this philosophy is already inside you.

Boredomism simply gives a name, a shape, and a gentle voice to something you've felt but couldn't express. It invites you to make peace with boredom—not as an enemy, but as a long-lost companion returning home.

CHAPTER FOUR

FINAL WORDS BEFORE YOU BEGIN

Before you turn the page and begin this inward journey, take a moment to pause—not out of obligation, but out of openness. This book does not demand a specific belief, nor does it require mastery. All it asks is your presence. Not the performative kind, but the quiet, honest kind that sits with questions without rushing toward conclusions.

You do not need to agree with everything written here. Boredomism is not a doctrine; it's a lens. A way to re-see the things you already know but might have forgotten. The chapters ahead won't offer grand solutions or life hacks. They will offer space. Space to reflect, to reconsider, to feel what normally gets filtered out by the busyness of daily life.

You may find parts that comfort you and parts that challenge you. That's part of the process. Allow this book to meet you where you are. Read it slowly, or not at all in certain moments. Reread pages that stir something inside you. Skip ahead or linger longer—it's all welcome here.

In the spirit of Boredomism, there is no rush. No finish line. Just a quiet unfolding, one page at a time. Let this be not just a book you read, but a book that accompanies you as you remember how to be.

Core Principles of Boredomism

This section introduces the foundational principles that give Boredomism its structure—not as rules, but as philosophical undercurrents. These principles are not linear commands, but lenses through which we learn to see our existence differently. Here, you'll meet the grounding truths that support "the art of doing nothing" in a noisy world.

There are three central principles we'll explore deeply:

1.   The Principle of Restorative Stillness
2.   The Principle of Effortless Presence
3.   The Principle of Quiet Awakening

Around them, we'll build chapters that unpack how these ideas apply emotionally, mentally, and existentially.

CHAPTER FIVE

THE CORE OF BOREDOMISM

At the heart of Boredomism lies a quiet revolution—the act of reclaiming the space to simply be. In a world designed to occupy every spare moment with stimulation, distraction, and achievement, the very idea of doing nothing feels radical, almost dangerous. But Boredomism argues that this "nothing" is not emptiness—it is the fertile ground of presence, healing, and rediscovery. The core belief is simple yet profound: boredom is not a void to be filled, but a space to be honored. It is not a failure of attention but a return to the self.

Boredomism is a philosophy built not on urgency, but on unhurried reflection. It does not reject action or ambition but questions their domination over every moment of life. It teaches that slowness is not laziness, and stillness is not passivity. Instead, both are forms of deep listening—to one's body, mind, and environment. When we stop running from boredom, we discover that it has something to say. It is often through these quiet, unstructured moments that creativity, clarity, and emotional truth rise to the surface.

This philosophy seeks to reframe the way we engage with time. It asks: what if we didn't try to fill every gap in our day? What if those gaps were actually where life happens in its purest form? In this way, Boredomism is an invitation back to the present. It strips away the pressure to be constantly productive or constantly entertained and invites us into a gentler, more meaningful rhythm of existence—one where presence is more valuable than progress, and where being is more celebrated than becoming.

The core of Boredomism is not about retreating from life—it is about meeting life in its raw, unfiltered form. It is about shedding the layers of noise, expectation, and motion that keep us from encountering our inner world. Through stillness, presence, and quiet awakening, Boredomism offers not a path to escape reality, but a way to fall back into it—more alert, more grounded, and more alive. It tells us that what we are searching for in the noise has been waiting patiently in the silence all along.

CHAPTER SIX

THE PRINCIPLE OF RESTORATIVE STILLNESS

In the cacophony of the modern world, stillness is no longer a luxury but a necessity. The Principle of Restorative Stillness recognizes that doing nothing is not equivalent to being idle; rather, it is a radical act of self-preservation. In a culture that worships productivity, taking a deliberate pause is revolutionary. Boredomism sees this pause not as stagnation but as a space for the soul to recover from overstimulation.

Restorative Stillness invites us to sit in silence, away from screens and schedules, and simply observe. As our senses settle, the nervous system calms, and the body remembers its natural rhythm. This principle honors the biological need for slowness, the psychological need for quiet, and the spiritual need for depth. Doing nothing, in this context, becomes a profound act of healing.

Historically, many spiritual traditions revered stillness. Monks, mystics, and sages withdrew from society not to escape life but to encounter it more fully. Boredomism reclaims this wisdom without the religious framework. It does not demand monastic isolation but encourages intentional stillness in everyday life.

For the modern individual, practicing stillness may begin with small rituals: sitting quietly for five minutes, watching the sky, or simply lying in bed without reaching for the phone. These micro-moments rebuild our internal balance and sharpen our awareness. What seems unproductive is, in fact, deeply regenerative.

Ultimately, Restorative Stillness is the ground zero of Boredomism. It offers an antidote to the restless striving that defines our age. It tells us that we do not have to earn our right to exist. We already do. In stillness, we remember.

CHAPTER SEVEN

THE PRINCIPLE OF EFFORTLESS PRESENCE

Effortlessness is often misunderstood. In a world driven by hustle, presence has become another item on the to-do list. The Principle of Effortless Presence challenges this notion by asserting that true presence arises not from effort, but from surrender. To be present, one must stop trying and start allowing.

This principle is deeply tied to the essence of Boredomism. When one is bored, there is a natural tendency to escape—to distract, to seek stimulation. But what happens when we simply stay? When we don't fight boredom but let it envelop us? Presence, quiet and clear, begins to emerge.

Effortless Presence invites us to experience the now without manipulation. Not every moment needs to be optimized or made meaningful. A leaf fluttering, the ticking of a clock, the rhythm of breath—these become rich experiences when we stop seeking more.

Ironically, when we try too hard to be present, we are no longer present. We are performing presence, not living it. Boredomism encourages a passive receptivity. We watch, we listen, we notice—without forcing insight or enlightenment.

The beauty of this principle lies in its simplicity. No special tools, training, or rituals are needed. Just the willingness to sit, to stay, and to be. In that state, life reveals its subtle layers. Effortless Presence is not an escape from life; it is life, unadorned and honest.

CHAPTER EIGHT

THE PRINCIPLE OF QUIET AWAKENING

Awakening is often portrayed as a dramatic transformation. But under Boredomism, it is a quiet unfolding. The Principle of Quiet Awakening suggests that personal growth does not always require intensity. Sometimes, it arrives in silence, slowly and softly.

When we give ourselves to boredom without resistance, we open the door to this awakening. In the absence of distraction, we start to hear the inner stirrings that usually get drowned out. Thoughts that once seemed trivial gain significance. Feelings we ignored start speaking clearly.

This principle teaches us to respect the subtle. It argues that transformation does not have to be loud. Just as the dawn doesn't explode but eases into daylight, so too does the self awaken gently. Boredom becomes the stage upon which this quiet drama unfolds.

Quiet Awakening is about clarity. When the noise settles, what remains is truth. That truth might be uncomfortable or liberating, but it is always real. Boredom allows us to meet ourselves without masks.

In this chapter, the reader is invited to treat boredom as a mirror. What do you see when you stop running? What surfaces when silence stretches out? Often, what we discover is not new, but long forgotten. And in remembering, we awaken.

CHAPTER NINE

BREAKING THE ILLUSIONS OF MODERN LIVING

In the noise and speed of modern life, we've inherited countless assumptions—about productivity, happiness, success, and even our own worth. These assumptions, repeated often enough, become invisible truths. We chase them without question, exhausting ourselves in the process. But what if these "truths" are illusions? What if the things we're told to pursue are actually the very things pulling us away from peace, meaning, and authenticity?

Boredomism offers a radical pause—a space to re-examine these cultural myths and emotional habits. In this chapter, we'll explore the deeper patterns driving our restlessness: the myth of constant becoming, the discomfort we avoid, the productivity we worship, and the fatigue we carry. Each subtopic offers a chance to break through illusion and reclaim a simpler, truer way of being.

1. The Illusion of Constant Becoming
   The modern world sells us a dream of endless self-improvement. There is always another goal to reach, another part of ourselves to fix. The Illusion of Constant Becoming is the lie that we must be in a perpetual state of growth to be valuable. Boredomism

calls this bluff.

This principle challenges the obsession with productivity and transformation. It recognizes the psychological toll of constant becoming: burnout, anxiety, and existential fatigue. Boredomism asks, what if we stopped trying to become and started being?

The illusion stems from fear—fear of stagnation, of insignificance, of irrelevance. But true meaning doesn't lie in ceaseless motion. Sometimes, staying where you are is the bravest act. To sit with who you are, without rushing to change, is to embrace your inherent worth.

This chapter explores the concept of "enoughness." It suggests that identity doesn't need constant renovation. Just like nature rests in winter, humans too must have seasons of stillness. In boredom, we find permission to be unfinished and yet whole.

Boredomism offers an alternative to the self-help hamster wheel. You are not a project. You are a presence. And your presence, even in silence, is enough. Constant becoming is an illusion; your being is real.

2. Discomfort as a Portal

Discomfort is not a sign of failure; it is often a sign of approaching truth. In Boredomism, the feeling of discomfort that emerges in boredom is a gateway to insight. When we first stop all motion, distraction, and noise, the mind resists. It itches for something—anything—to fill the gap.

This chapter explores how boredom exposes emotional sediment. Things we've buried under tasks and distractions begin to rise. At first, this feels unsettling. But instead of escaping it, Boredomism asks us to remain. In that discomfort lies clarity, healing, and reconnection.

The science behind this principle reveals that our brain, when deprived of stimulation, begins to process backlog emotions and unresolved thoughts. This is not dysfunction; it is detox. It is the nervous system recalibrating after overstimulation.

Boredom, then, is like a gentle shaking of the internal snow globe. At first, things swirl and visibility drops. But if you wait, clarity returns. This emotional visibility allows us to see not only ourselves but life more truthfully. It takes courage, but it's worth it.

To go through discomfort is to reenter your body, your truth, and your silence. Discomfort isn't a warning; it's an invitation. In Boredomism, we walk through this portal and come out more whole.

3. The Collapse of the Productivity Myth

Productivity is the golden calf of modern life. It promises success, happiness, and worth. But more often than not, it delivers burnout, alienation, and a shallow sense of purpose. This chapter addresses the core lie: that we are only valuable when producing.

Boredomism radically repositions value. It asserts that being—not doing—is sufficient. It critiques the cultural inheritance that ties identity to output. In truth, many of our most meaningful experiences—love, beauty, presence—require no productivity.

We explore the roots of the productivity myth, tracing it from the Industrial Revolution to the digital age. Work ethic became a moral standard, and rest a sin. Boredomism dismantles that narrative.

Instead, we begin to view rest, reflection, and stillness as valid modes of living. The chapter gives examples of people and cultures who resist productivity worship—monastics, slow-living advocates, and artists.

In reclaiming non-productivity, we find spaciousness. We find ourselves. Boredom becomes not a block to purpose, but the soil from which authentic purpose grows.

4. Mental Fatigue and the Nervous System

Modern life is not just busy—it is exhausting. From the constant influx of notifications to the expectation of always being "on," our minds rarely get the rest they need. Mental fatigue has become the silent epidemic of our time. Boredomism approaches this issue through a neuropsychological lens, recognizing boredom not as laziness but as a natural signal of cognitive overload.

When the brain is overstimulated, it loses its ability to filter and prioritize information effectively. This leads to a kind of internal traffic jam—thoughts and emotions all pushing to the forefront, none getting processed properly. In boredom, however, the noise begins to recede. The Principle of Restorative Stillness acts as a reset mechanism, giving the nervous system a chance to return to homeostasis.

We often forget that the brain, like the body, requires intervals of rest to function optimally. Research shows that moments of "doing nothing" stimulate the brain's default mode network—a system responsible for memory consolidation, creative problem-solving, and self-awareness. Boredom, in this light, is not a breakdown but a reboot.

This chapter highlights how deliberately embracing boredom can reduce symptoms of anxiety, improve sleep quality, and enhance emotional regulation. The parasympathetic nervous system—the body's rest-and-digest mode—is activated when we cease activity, allowing deep repair to take place.

By shifting our perception of mental fatigue from something shameful to something sacred, Boredomism gives us permission to slow down without guilt. Mental clarity is not found through effort, but through surrender. Boredom becomes the doorway to deep neurological healing.

5. The Fear of Missing Out (FOMO)

FOMO, or the fear of missing out, is one of the most corrosive illusions of the digital age. It keeps us scrolling, comparing, chasing experiences we don't even truly desire. It feeds on the anxiety that life is happening elsewhere, and that we must stay plugged in to avoid irrelevance. Boredomism disrupts this myth by redefining what it means to be fully alive.

When we embrace the present moment—even when it's empty, even when it's still—we begin to loosen FOMO's grip. The quiet space we often avoid turns out to be the only place where we can actually encounter life as it is. Instead of fearing what we're missing, we begin to value what we're witnessing.

This chapter challenges the idea that meaning only exists in the dramatic, the eventful, the shared. Boredom teaches us that the mundane, the quiet, and the unshared moments are no less meaningful. Watching a shadow move across the floor or sipping tea alone can be an act of deep presence.

FOMO thrives on the belief that value lies elsewhere. Boredomism turns that belief inside out. It insists that the here and now, when attended to with presence, is complete. We do not miss life by being still; we find it.

The antidote to FOMO is not more engagement, but deeper attention. In embracing boredom, we discover that nothing is missing—not really. We are not missing out; we are missing in.

6. Relearning How to be Alone

Solitude is no longer a default human experience. In an age of constant connection, being alone has become something to be feared or fixed. Yet solitude is foundational to self-knowledge. Boredomism revives solitude not as isolation but as an essential practice of personal integration.

To be alone without distraction is to meet yourself—perhaps for the first time. Without others to mirror us, we must look inward. And in doing so, we uncover parts of ourselves we've long ignored or forgotten. This chapter explores how intentional solitude allows for self-reflection, emotional clarity, and creative thinking.

We examine historical examples of solitude—from Thoreau at Walden Pond to the silent retreats of Zen practitioners—and how these moments were not about withdrawal but revelation. The point is not to be antisocial, but to become more authentic in our social presence by knowing ourselves first.

Many avoid solitude because it is uncomfortable. But discomfort, as Boredomism suggests, is not the enemy. It is the invitation. In boredom and solitude, we are given a chance to be real, unfiltered, and whole. We shed performance and remember presence.

Relearning how to be alone is not just about physical separation. It's about mental and emotional self-containment. Boredom teaches us that we don't need to be entertained to be at peace. In fact, peace begins where entertainment ends.

7. The Still Space Between Thoughts

Most of our lives are spent bouncing from one thought to another like stepping stones across a river. Rarely do we pause in between. But what if those empty spaces—the gaps between thoughts—are where our deepest truths reside? This chapter explores the underappreciated terrain of mental silence.

Boredomism views the still space between thoughts as the gateway to intuitive knowing. In this space, we are not analyzing or reacting. We are simply aware. It's a mode of consciousness that is less about thinking and more about being. Meditation traditions have long recognized this, but Boredomism approaches it through the accessible lens of everyday life.

When we stop trying to fill our minds, we notice these pockets of silence. They often occur when we are bored—waiting in line, lying in bed, or sitting alone with no tasks. Rather than rushing to fill the silence, we are invited to remain in it.

This still space is fertile ground. Creativity, insight, and emotional clarity often bubble up here, not through force, but through openness. Boredom, by slowing the pace of thought, creates the perfect conditions for this awareness to emerge.

Instead of fearing emptiness, Boredomism reveres it. The space between thoughts is not a void—it is a source. And within it, we find a kind of wisdom that no book or teacher can give us. We just have to be still enough to listen.

8. Choosing Less in a World That Demands More

We live in a culture of excess—more goals, more success, more connectivity. But this constant demand for "more" comes at a cost: our peace, our clarity, our presence. Boredomism dares to propose the opposite. What if less is not a loss, but a liberation?

Choosing less doesn't mean opting out of life. It means choosing what truly matters and letting the rest fall away. This chapter dives into the minimalist aspect of Boredomism—not as an aesthetic, but as a philosophy of attention. When we choose less, we give more attention to what remains.

Boredom becomes the moment where we re-evaluate. When we stop doing, we start noticing what we actually want. The silence shows us the noise we've mistaken for necessity. We begin to discern the difference between impulse and intention.

This principle also extends to consumption, commitments, and emotional bandwidth. Choosing fewer possessions, fewer distractions, and fewer demands can open the door to deeper living. In boredom, we create space—not just in time, but in heart and mind.

Ultimately, this chapter is about empowerment. Choosing less is not deprivation; it's self-respect. Boredomism reframes minimalism as not just a lifestyle, but a path to meaning. The less we carry, the further we go—and the lighter we feel.

Philosophy in Motion: Practicing Boredomism

The power of a philosophy lies not only in its ideas but in how deeply it can be lived. This part of the book is where Boredomism steps down from the abstract and enters the personal. Now that we've understood the essence of stillness, presence, and quiet awakening, we ask: how do we live this? How do we welcome boredom not just as a concept, but as a rhythm—a daily presence in our lives?

Practicing Boredomism doesn't mean meditating for hours or giving up technology. It means learning to see the value in pauses, to treat silence as a companion, and to choose presence over performance. It means recognizing the sacred in the simple, and the profound in the ordinary. It is not about escapism but deep engagement with the unnoticed layers of life. These chapters will guide you through the lived form of Boredomism: in your schedule, your screen habits, your breath, your time, and even your creativity. It is about being differently in the world.

In this modern world, the temptation to fill every gap is strong. We are constantly fed the illusion that productivity is purpose, that stimulation is joy, and that silence is void. Boredomism breaks this illusion not through resistance, but through radical softness. It offers not a rejection of the world, but a reorientation within it—a new relationship with time, attention, and inner spaciousness.

This part of the book invites you to explore what it means to practice boredom—not as a flaw to correct but as a form of wisdom to cultivate. You will not be given rules or rigid schedules.

Instead, you will encounter living invitations: to pause, to watch, to feel, and to return. These chapters are about planting small seeds—tiny, intentional moments where boredom becomes a teacher.

Philosophy in motion is not movement for the sake of movement. It is movement that emerges from stillness. The chapters that follow will guide you through everyday practices that embody Boredomism. From reclaiming micro-moments to rebuilding your sense of time, each chapter offers both a philosophical lens and a lived path forward.

In the noise of the world, we are rarely taught how to listen. In the speed of life, we forget how to arrive. This part of the book is your space to re-learn both. To move gently. To notice the quiet. To let your boredom become not something to endure, but something to explore. Let this be the beginning of walking Boredomism—not in grand gestures, but in the smallest, most meaningful ways.

CHAPTER TEN

THE PHILOSOPHY OF SMALL SPACES

In a world built for movement, we often overlook the power of stillness—not just in long meditations or weekend retreats, but in the smallest spaces of our day. The Philosophy of Small Spaces is about reclaiming those micro-moments we usually discard or rush through. Waiting for a page to load. Standing in a grocery line. Sitting in a parked car before stepping out. These are often the first places boredom appears—and the first chances we have to embrace it.

Our minds are conditioned to fill these spaces. We reach for our phones, open tabs, scroll mindlessly, or mentally plan the next hour. But boredomism invites us to do something radical in those moments: nothing at all. Not because doing nothing is inherently better—but because it reveals something that doing often hides. That emptiness you feel? That subtle restlessness? That's where your real self begins to speak.

Small spaces aren't about size—they're about silence. They are the pockets of unoccupied time that exist between the "main events" of life. The Philosophy of Small Spaces encourages us to pay attention to these neglected intervals and to discover the richness that lives within them. When we resist the urge to distract ourselves, we begin to notice details: the rhythm of our breath, the stillness around us, the fleeting nature of our thoughts. These moments become soft mirrors.

This practice also reconnects us with our internal tempo—which is often much slower than the tempo the world demands of us. By honoring small spaces, we recalibrate. Instead of racing ahead mentally, we sync with the actual pace of life. A boiling kettle becomes more than waiting. A crosswalk countdown becomes more than delay. These fragments of time become fields of awareness.

There's no need to restructure your day or isolate yourself. You don't need a special room, a candle, or an hour of uninterrupted silence. The practice of boredomism begins exactly where you are. Try this: The next time you're about to fill a gap with your phone or thoughts, stop. Let the moment hang. Watch it unfold without rushing it. You don't need to do anything. Just be present. Boredom might appear—but let it. It's not there to punish you. It's there to restore you.

In learning to be present in small spaces, we build a habit of self-trust. We learn that we don't have to be busy to be valid. We don't have to be thinking to be awake. We don't have to be moving to be alive. And in those spaces, without realizing it, we begin the slow and quiet art of coming home to ourselves.

CHAPTER ELEVEN

Doing Nothing with Intent

In a culture that glorifies productivity, the phrase "doing nothing" sounds like a waste. It carries a stigma—one that suggests laziness, lack of ambition, or irresponsibility. But Boredomism turns that judgment on its head. Doing nothing, when done with intent, becomes a sacred act. It is a practice of pausing not because you have nothing to do, but because you are choosing not to do for a while.

This chapter is not about abandonment of all responsibility. It is about reclaiming a space within your day—or your life—that is free from external demands and internal pressure. It's not about shutting down. It's about waking up... slowly, quietly, and without performance. When we approach nothingness deliberately, we open the doorway to presence in its purest, most unforced form.

Doing nothing with intent means putting the phone down without needing to pick up a book. It means resisting the urge to turn "free time" into a new project. It means allowing a stretch of time—ten minutes or an entire afternoon—where your value is not tied to what you produce. The shift is not in what you do, but in how you see what you're not doing. You begin to notice your breath. Your surroundings. The micro-thoughts that usually get lost in noise.

Intentional non-doing doesn't mean your mind will be blank. In fact, it often becomes more alive. The practice isn't about creating silence; it's about noticing what's already there beneath the surface. You may encounter discomfort at first—the twitch to reach for a task, the creeping guilt of idleness. That's the residue of a world that taught you to only exist when you're useful. Stay with it. That unease is your system adjusting to a slower rhythm, not failing.

Many spiritual and philosophical traditions embrace a version of this practice: from the Zen concept of wu wei (effortless action) to the Christian tradition of contemplative prayer to the secular idea of "mental still time." Boredomism removes the formalities and invites this way of being into your regular life. You don't need a retreat. You don't need a guru. You need space, and the courage to let it stay empty for a while.

This chapter isn't meant to be prescriptive. Rather, it asks you to explore: What might your version of doing nothing look like? Maybe it's sitting with tea and letting your thoughts settle. Maybe it's watching light move across the floor. Maybe it's staring out a window without narration. The key is not in the activity—or lack of it—but in the intention to release your grip on productivity for a moment.

Doing nothing with intent becomes an act of quiet rebellion. In those moments, you are no longer a consumer, a performer, or a cog in someone else's system. You are simply a person—breathing, observing, and existing—without needing to earn your existence. And that, in a world of constant noise, might be the most meaningful thing you do all day.

CHAPTER TWELVE

THE DIGITAL DILEMMA

We are more connected than any generation before us, and yet, we are also more distracted, more anxious, and more mentally scattered. This is the paradox at the heart of the digital dilemma. We carry in our hands an endless stream of entertainment, communication, and information, but with it comes a subtle erosion of presence, attention, and mental stillness. Boredom, once a natural rhythm of human experience, is now treated as an error to be corrected instantly—with a scroll, a click, a swipe.

Boredomism doesn't ask us to abandon technology, but it does ask us to reconsider our relationship with it. Our devices are not inherently harmful. The dilemma lies in our reflexive dependence on them—how we reach for them in every moment of pause, how they fill the quiet before we can even recognize it as valuable. This compulsion disrupts the very possibility of doing nothing. The moment we might encounter boredom, we are already pulling ourselves away from it.

Every time we avoid boredom with a digital distraction, we close the door on an opportunity for awareness. That tiny window of stillness—a moment in the car, the time waiting in line, a silent afternoon—is consumed by noise before it can become meaningful. We've traded our inner landscape for external stimulation. We scroll to avoid discomfort, refresh to escape emptiness, and binge to suppress presence. But in doing so, we miss the hidden gifts of those very spaces we keep trying to skip.

The digital dilemma is not about evil screens—it's about the loss of intentional engagement. We no longer choose what to consume. Algorithms choose for us. And boredom, which once served as a reset button for the mind, is now something we rarely experience long enough to even understand. When everything is available all the time, we lose our ability to sit with the unavailable—the silence, the subtle, the slow.

Boredomism offers a radical shift: what if we didn't fill those moments? What if we allowed a digital pause—not out of restriction, but out of reverence for the space that boredom offers? A five-minute gap without reaching for the phone becomes not an empty hole, but a quiet portal back to ourselves. In that space, creativity stirs. Emotions rise. Thoughtfulness returns. These are not distractions from life—they are life.

We are not asked to give up technology entirely. But we are challenged to return to boredom on purpose. This means letting there be gaps in the day. It means putting down the device not as a punishment, but as an opening. Try not checking your phone in a waiting room. Try eating without a screen. Try waking up and simply lying in bed for a few extra minutes, doing absolutely nothing. These are the modern rituals of Boredomism. They don't ask for control or strict rules—just awareness, just intention.

When we reclaim boredom, we reclaim attention. And when we reclaim attention, we begin to see how much of ourselves we had outsourced to the digital world. Boredomism doesn't tell us to run from technology—but it reminds us that the most valuable notifications come from within.

CHAPTER THIRTEEN

RECONSTRUCTING TIME

Time is no longer something we live within. It's something we try to control, conquer, manage, and optimize. We divide it into tasks, schedule it to the minute, and punish ourselves when we "waste" it. In this modern framework, time has been reduced to a currency—a resource to spend wisely. But in the philosophy of Boredomism, we reject that view entirely. Time, we believe, is not something to dominate. It is something to enter.

Boredomism reimagines time not as a strict, linear structure but as a fluid, lived experience—one that changes shape based on our presence. When you're truly engaged in stillness or non-doing, minutes feel like hours. When you're immersed in overstimulation, hours disappear in seconds. In both cases, the clock hasn't changed—but your relationship to time has. This relationship is what must be reconstructed if we are to reclaim life's natural rhythm.

Modern timekeeping—rooted in industrialism, capitalism, and efficiency—trains us to equate productivity with worth. We feel the ticking of the clock like pressure, not presence. We ask, "How much can I do in a day?" instead of, "How much of this day did I actually feel?" Boredomism shifts that focus. It asks us to move from tracking time to experiencing it. This reconstruction begins not by changing what we do, but by how we move through time.

To live with time rather than against it means learning to trust in unmeasured moments. For example, imagine sitting on a park bench with nothing planned. You're not waiting for someone. You're not checking your phone. You're just watching. Ten minutes stretch. The wind brushes your face. You remember something old and tender. You feel. You shift. You return. That is real time. Time that breathes with you, rather than collapses under you.

Boredom is often where we meet this kind of time. It creates a crack in the rigid structure of modern life. When we stop doing and simply observe, we suddenly notice time again. We feel its pace. We watch how slow it can move—and instead of resenting that, we begin to respect it. We begin to see that slowness doesn't rob us of meaning. It reveals it. It lets things emerge that we usually rush past: subtle thoughts, unprocessed emotions, natural creativity, and calm.

The emotional impact of this shift is profound. People who reconstruct their relationship with time often describe feeling less anxious, more patient, and less reactive. It's not that life slows down—it's that they slow down, and so they begin to live more of life. And here lies a central truth of Boredomism: when we stop speeding through time, time begins to feed us instead of deplete us.

There's also a spiritual dimension. Many ancient traditions speak of "timelessness" or "eternal presence." But Boredomism doesn't require spiritual belief. Instead, it suggests that when we are fully immersed in a moment—especially a still one—time dissolves. Not because it vanishes, but because our sense of urgency does. We realize there is no better time to be than now. Not because now is amazing, but because it simply is.

Reconstructing time also means reconstructing value. When you stop measuring the worth of a day by how much you did, you start measuring it by how much you noticed. Was there silence? Was there breath? Did you feel your life while it was happening? Boredom gives you access to these measures, not by making time stop, but by letting you fall back into its natural flow.

In practical terms, this may look like protecting moments of unstructured time. Letting your mornings unfold slowly. Not setting alarms on weekends. Walking without headphones. Watching the sun go down without photographing it. These moments rewire your sense of what time is for. You begin to feel not that you own time, but that you are part of it—just as trees grow in it, and clouds move through it, and oceans breathe in rhythm with the moon.

To reconstruct time is not to abandon plans or schedules altogether. It is to stop worshipping them. It is to place them back where they belong: as tools, not masters. Boredomism doesn't call for disorganization—it calls for sovereignty over the one thing you can never get back. And that sovereignty is born the moment you stop measuring time in tasks and begin living it in stillness.

You were not born to race time. You were born to move with it. To feel the slow days and the still afternoons as not interruptions, but as offerings. Boredom, when allowed to unfold naturally, reconstructs your time not just by changing your calendar—but by changing your pace, your priorities, and your presence.

CHAPTER FOURTEEN

THE FERTILE VOID

We've been conditioned to believe that only filled spaces are valuable—spaces packed with information, activity, or noise. Emptiness, by contrast, is seen as a problem to fix, an inefficiency, or at best, an intermission. But Boredomism invites a different perspective: that emptiness can be sacred. That in still, open, and unfilled spaces, something deeper grows. This is the essence of the fertile void—the idea that nothingness is not lifeless, but full of unseen potential.

The fertile void is not the same as apathy, stagnation, or depression. It is a spacious openness—a moment in which we are no longer reaching for the next thing. The to-do list is not in front of us. The screens are off. The mind begins to settle. And in that space where we're not trying to be anything, do anything, or prove anything, we start to feel something stir. This is the gentle undercurrent of becoming—not the frantic kind, but the quiet type that occurs when the soil lies fallow.

In nature, the fallow field is not abandoned. It is left untouched to restore its nutrients, to breathe, to return to balance. Farmers understand this instinctively. But in modern life, we've forgotten the wisdom of stillness. We never stop planting, never stop producing, and then we wonder why nothing meaningful grows. The fertile void teaches us that pausing is not just helpful—it is necessary. Boredom, far from being an obstacle, becomes the womb of new thought.

When we stop filling every moment, we make space for something original. Creative insight, deep emotional processing, even subtle spiritual experiences rarely arrive in crowded mental spaces. They need room. But room doesn't just mean time—it means mental quiet, an absence of urgency. The fertile void is where those deeper truths slip in—not through force, but through invitation. It's where creativity is not summoned but allowed.

We often think of inspiration as something to chase, to manufacture, or to hunt down. But inspiration is shy. It does not scream over noise. It waits for us to sit down, unplug, and get bored enough to notice it. Many of the world's most profound ideas, inventions, and artworks emerged not from busyness but from silence—those long, slow hours where the mind wandered freely. The fertile void is not productive in the traditional sense, but it is generative in the deepest one.

Sitting in this kind of stillness can be uncomfortable at first. The mind will want to escape. The body will itch to do something. But if you stay, if you don't rush to fill the space, something begins to shift. You may begin to notice faint thoughts rising—half-formed memories, odd questions, strange but meaningful images. You're not "meditating" in the traditional sense. You're simply sitting in creative waiting. And that waiting, if trusted, often becomes a channel for truth.

To live with awareness of the fertile void is to resist the fear of inactivity. It is to trust that something of value can grow even when it looks like nothing is happening. In this way, boredom becomes not a burden, but a field of invitation—a place where what's meant to surface, does. Whether it's an idea, a feeling, or simply the peace of having nothing to do, it all arises from the same root: space. Space without agenda. Stillness without pressure. Silence with presence.

Ultimately, the fertile void is not a technique—it is a posture. A willingness to stay open. A choice to stop interfering with the moment and let it breathe. Boredomism invites us to make friends with these empty spaces. To see them not as problems, but as possibilities. Because in the end, it is often from nothing that the most beautiful and necessary things are born.

CHAPTER FIFTEEN

SITTING WITHOUT SEEKING: MEDITATION AS A BOREDOMIST PRACTICE

Meditation, as it's commonly understood today, is often tangled in expectations—calm the mind, control the breath, reach mindfulness, become more productive. Even in rest, we are taught to aim for something. But Boredomism does not chase results. It doesn't seek mental clarity, emotional mastery, or even peace. Instead, it allows for a radically different approach: sitting without seeking.

This practice is not meditation as a technique. It is not meant to be optimized, tracked, or improved upon. It is simply a return to stillness—not to fix the mind, but to let it breathe. In Boredomism, we don't sit to escape thoughts or transcend discomfort. We sit to witness them. We sit not to empty the mind, but to stop adding more. To be exactly where we are, without editing the moment.

In this way, sitting becomes a symbolic expression of the philosophy itself: the art of doing nothing on purpose. It asks for no special posture, no chant, no breath pattern. Just the willingness to be present without shaping the experience. If the mind races, that's fine. If you feel distracted, that too is allowed. In Boredomism, even mental chaos has a place.

The true gift of this kind of sitting is that it welcomes whatever shows up. You may find calm, or you may feel more agitated than before. You may uncover a thought that surprises you, or feel nothing at all. What matters is not what arises—but that you stayed. That you resisted the urge to fill, fix, or flee the silence. In that decision to stay, something deep begins to shift. Not as an achievement, but as an emergence.

Often, the discomfort that surfaces in silence is simply the backlog of sensations we've repressed. When we stop numbing ourselves with motion, content, or stimulation, the raw truth of our mental and emotional state rises to the surface. This is not failure—it is exposure. And it is necessary. Boredomism honors this exposure. It understands that healing begins not when the pain goes away, but when we stop running from it.

In a culture obsessed with control, stillness becomes the last untamed territory. This kind of meditative non-doing returns you to it. When you sit without trying to fix or improve yourself, the nervous system begins to trust again. Your body doesn't feel coerced into performance. Your mind doesn't brace itself for judgment. The space becomes safe. And within that safety, your presence deepens—not through focus, but through allowance.

This sitting is not about discipline. You're not required to do it daily. There is no measure of progress. You can sit for ten minutes, twenty, or even just two. What matters is the spirit of the practice: that you sit with nothing to prove, nowhere to get, and no outcome to reach. In this way, it's not even meditation—it's just being. Being still, being here, being enough.

You might call this a practice, but it's really a return. A quiet homecoming. And as you continue to explore Boredomism, this simple act of sitting without seeking becomes a kind of anchor. Not to still the storm, but to learn how to sit within it—untouched, undemanding, unafraid.

The Resistance Within

Every philosophy that touches the core of human nature eventually meets resistance—not just from society, but from within ourselves. Stillness might sound peaceful, but for many, it feels unbearable. Silence can seem heavy. Doing nothing can stir discomfort, fear, guilt, even shame.

This part of the book addresses those reactions. It does not aim to remove them, but to understand them. These chapters walk through the psychological, emotional, and cultural friction that arises when we try to live differently in a world addicted to noise and motion.

Boredomism, at its core, invites not just contemplation—but confrontation. Here, we look closely at the thoughts that whisper, "You're falling behind," and "You should be doing more." We name those voices. We sit with them. And in time, we begin to see them for what they are—not truths, but habits. Not insights, but echoes.

CHAPTER SIXTEEN

The Guilt of Inactivity

It's a strange thing, the guilt we feel when we stop. Not guilt for hurting someone or doing something wrong—but for simply pausing, for resting, for doing... nothing. Inactivity has become a kind of sin in modern culture. It carries with it a silent shame, a haunting whisper that says: You should be doing more. This guilt is not born from laziness, but from centuries of conditioning. We've been taught that our worth is tied to output, to effort, to constant engagement. And when we dare to step outside that cycle, guilt arrives like an alarm bell.

Boredomism confronts this guilt head-on. It recognizes that the problem is not the pause itself, but the internalized belief that rest must be earned. That slowness must be justified. That stopping equals falling behind. In truth, this guilt is not moral—it's manufactured. It's the byproduct of systems that benefit from our exhaustion. Productivity culture, capitalism, even parts of modern self-help rhetoric—they all promote motion as virtue. Doing nothing, then, becomes suspicious. A problem to be fixed.

The irony is that many of us don't even enjoy our busyness. We crave rest. We long for stillness. And yet, when we finally get a chance to stop, we don't feel relief—we feel unworthy. This is not a natural reaction. It's an implanted narrative. We've been programmed to believe that stillness is weakness. That rest is failure. That time spent in quiet reflection is time wasted. Boredomism invites us to unlearn all of that. It doesn't just tell us to slow down—it asks why slowing down feels wrong in the first place.

The guilt of inactivity is deeply emotional. It shows up in subtle ways. A fidgeting discomfort when you sit too long without checking your phone. A pang of unease when you take a day off and don't accomplish anything "useful." A voice that says, You should be doing something. This voice doesn't belong to you. It's an echo of a world that only knows how to measure value by movement. And the only way to quiet it is to question it—again and again.

Boredomism proposes a shift: what if doing nothing wasn't a failure of discipline, but a triumph of awareness? What if stopping wasn't falling behind, but finally catching up—with yourself, your breath, your presence? To live by this idea takes courage. It means risking judgment. It means letting go of the pride that comes from busyness and embracing the vulnerability of simply being. It means allowing space in your life that serves no purpose other than to exist.

There will be moments when the guilt returns. You will wonder if you're wasting your time, falling short, being irresponsible. Let it come. Let it rise. But don't let it drive. Instead, observe it. Name it. Say: This is not mine. This is the voice of a world that forgot how to rest. And then return—to the chair, the silence, the stillness. You do not have to fight the guilt. You only have to sit beside it without moving. Eventually, it will tire. And you will remain.

In time, what once felt like guilt becomes grace. The space that once scared you becomes sacred. The act of doing nothing begins to feel not like giving up, but like returning. Returning to yourself. To presence. To the quiet truth that you are not here to be constantly useful. You are here to be awake. And sometimes, the most awake thing you can do is stop.

CHAPTER SEVENTEEN

STILLNESS AND SHAME

Stillness may appear serene from the outside—but for many, it awakens something heavy on the inside. The moment we stop moving, producing, achieving, or entertaining, a strange discomfort can rise—not just restlessness, but something deeper. A feeling of being undeserving of that quiet. A weight in the chest. An echoing thought: "You should be doing something."

That feeling has a name. Shame.

It's a quiet, often invisible emotion, rooted in the belief that our worth depends on what we do. And when we choose stillness—when we decide not to do—we are suddenly stripped of that external validation. There are no metrics, no praise, no progress to measure. And in that absence, shame begins to speak.

Shame tells us we're lazy. That we're falling behind. That others are pushing forward while we're stuck. It might whisper, "If you were stronger, more focused, more ambitious, you wouldn't be sitting here doing nothing." The mind mistakes stillness for failure because it has never learned to see rest as valid.

But this response is not a personal flaw. It is a cultural inheritance. From a young age, we are taught that value is earned through doing. "Don't waste time." "Make something of yourself." "Stay busy." We internalize the idea that being isn't enough. That to pause is to fall. That silence is a void that must be filled. Shame thrives in this atmosphere—quietly shaping how we treat ourselves when we're not producing.

Stillness, in this sense, becomes threatening. It strips away distractions. It leaves us with nothing to hide behind. And in that moment of naked presence, we're faced with a question many of us spend years avoiding: "Am I enough without anything to show for it?"

Boredomism directly challenges this cultural wound. It proposes that your value is not tied to your activity. That worth is not earned through output. That you are not an assembly line, a content machine, or a walking résumé. You are a human being. And stillness is not your shame—it is your birthright.

To sit in stillness and feel shame rise is not a failure. It is a revealing. It's what happens when you begin peeling back the layers of performance you've been wearing for years. The guilt, the twitch to check your phone, the need to "just do one quick task"—these are not signs of laziness. They are signs of healing beginning.

This chapter is not here to shame your shame. It's here to hold space for it. To say: Yes, it's normal to feel this way. But you don't have to obey that feeling anymore. You can sit with it. Breathe with it. Let it pass through you. And in doing so, you are rewriting the inner code that says you must be useful to be lovable.

Over time, stillness can become your refuge instead of your trigger. But only if you walk through the discomfort—not around it. You may not like what stillness shows you at first. But that is the gift: stillness shows you what noise has hidden. And shame, once exposed to presence, loses its grip. Not overnight, but gradually. Like fog lifting in the morning sun.

So, the next time shame visits you in a moment of boredom, try not to resist it. Acknowledge it. Thank it, even—it's trying to protect a self-image you no longer need. And then return to your breath. Return to your seat. You are not broken for resting. You are returning to wholeness through it.

Stillness does not diminish you. It introduces you—to a version of yourself that does not perform for permission to exist.

CHAPTER EIGHTEEN

THE ADDICTION TO ACTION

There is a deep, often invisible addiction we carry—one more culturally accepted than alcohol, more praised than productivity, and more dangerous than it appears. It is the addiction to action. Not meaningful action, not movement with purpose—but motion for motion's sake. A constant state of doing, reacting, reaching, fixing, checking, planning, adjusting. It masquerades as ambition. It feels like progress. But at its core, it often stems from fear.

Fear of what might surface if we stop. Fear of appearing lazy. Fear of irrelevance. Fear that without constant activity, we might not exist at all. This addiction is socially reinforced: "Keep pushing." "Stay busy." "Hustle harder." We are applauded for burnout, praised for always being available, admired for exhaustion disguised as dedication.

But Boredomism calls this out for what it is: a subtle form of self-avoidance. When you are addicted to action, you are not just avoiding stillness—you are avoiding the version of yourself that can only be found in stillness. In your busyness, you never truly meet yourself. You just pass yourself by in the blur of tasks and distractions.

Let's be clear: action is not inherently bad. Movement can be beautiful. Building things, creating, engaging—these are all valuable. But the problem arises when action becomes unconscious, automatic, compulsive. When you wake up and already feel behind. When rest feels wasteful. When your self-worth is measured in output. That's no longer life. That's performance addiction.

Many people discover this only when they are forced to stop—through illness, burnout, heartbreak, or collapse. Only then do they realize how much of their identity was built on motion. Without the constant doing, they don't know who they are. And that's terrifying. This chapter is not about shaming that addiction. It's about naming it, facing it, and beginning the slow process of unhooking from it.

Stillness feels intolerable to someone addicted to doing. When a moment opens up—no plans, no noise, no tasks—the body tenses. The mind searches for something to solve. The hands reach for the phone. This is not laziness trying to be avoided—it is intimacy with the self trying to be postponed. Stillness is a mirror, and many aren't ready to look.

The addiction to action often begins in childhood. We're praised when we accomplish something, not when we rest. We're labeled "good" when we're busy, "bad" when we're idle. Over time, stillness becomes associated with shame. Rest feels like failure. And boredom, instead of being seen as potential space, is viewed as a personal flaw to be corrected.

To free ourselves from this cycle, Boredomism doesn't ask us to stop moving. It asks us to start noticing. Why are we doing what we're doing? What emotion lies beneath the urge to stay busy? Can we sit with the discomfort that arises when we put the to-do list down, even for ten minutes?

The healing begins not in the absence of action, but in the presence of awareness. When we do something, we ask ourselves gently: Is this needed? Is this nourishing? Or am I just avoiding something deeper? We begin to slow the pace, not to become less effective, but to become more aligned.

Some will argue that rest is a luxury—that slowing down is a privilege. And in many ways, they're right. But in another way, stillness is our birthright. You were not born to prove yourself through constant motion. You were born with the ability to pause, to breathe, to be. And reclaiming that ability—no matter how small—is a kind of liberation.

So what does it look like to begin breaking this addiction? You start by creating invitations to stillness, not forcing silence, but welcoming it. Take a walk without headphones. Let yourself be bored without fixing it. Pause in the middle of the day and do nothing—not because you've earned it, but because you exist. That's enough.

Boredomism doesn't promise instant comfort. In fact, the beginning is often harder than staying busy. But over time, something changes. You begin to trust the pause. You begin to feel safe without noise. You realize that doing less doesn't mean you are less. And in that realization, a whole new way of living opens up—one that is slower, deeper, and more free.

CHAPTER NINETEEN

BOREDOM VS DEPRESSION: UNDERSTANDING THE DIVIDE BETWEEN STILLNESS AND STAGNATION

One of the most common—and sensitive—misunderstandings about boredom is its confusion with depression. For many, the stillness that Boredomism invites can feel eerily close to emotional heaviness, numbness, or a deep lack of motivation. And that's a valid concern. This chapter exists to draw a careful, compassionate line between two very different inner states: the intentional pause of boredom and the emotional paralysis of depression.

Let's be clear: Boredom is not depression. But the two can feel adjacent, especially at the beginning of this practice. Depression is a clinical and emotional condition often marked by despair, disconnection, hopelessness, and a painful loss of vitality. It is not laziness. It is not weakness. And it is certainly not chosen.

Boredom, on the other hand, is often a gateway emotion—a neutral signal that space has been created, and the mind doesn't yet know what to do with it. In that way, it is the threshold, not the decline.

Stillness can trigger old patterns—especially for those who have experienced depression. When we slow down, things we've avoided begin to resurface: sadness, restlessness, loneliness, confusion. The lack of stimulation can feel like a void. But what makes Boredomism different is the intention behind the stillness. In Boredomism, you are choosing to stop. You are aware. You are observing. And you're doing so not because you're unable to act, but because you're consciously stepping back.

This chapter is not written to diagnose or treat depression, nor should Boredomism ever be seen as a replacement for therapy, medication, or professional care. But it can be part of the emotional landscape that helps us recognize when we are simply in the early stages of mental quiet—not descending into darkness. Often, what feels like emotional emptiness is actually a detox from constant stimulation, where meaning has yet to surface but safety has already begun.

Here's a helpful metaphor: boredom is like a room that's been emptied. At first, it feels blank and strange. You want to fill it. But if you sit in that room long enough, your eyes adjust. You begin to see the light on the walls. You begin to imagine what could grow there. Depression, however, is a room where the lights are off, the air is heavy, and the door feels locked. The difference is subtle, but real—and learning to distinguish them is one of the most important emotional skills a person can develop.

Another difference lies in energy. In boredom, there is often a quiet aliveness beneath the surface—even if small. A part of you is watching, wondering, listening. You may feel restless, but you are still engaged. In depression, energy tends to collapse inward. Even basic tasks feel impossible. The self becomes unreachable. If boredom asks, "What now?", depression whispers, "Why bother?"—and that difference matters.

Boredomism does not deny emotional pain. In fact, it encourages you to meet it head-on. But it does so with support—with structure, language, and an invitation to witness, rather than surrender to, discomfort. When practiced with care, boredom can actually be a bridge out of depressive habits—not by forcing happiness, but by offering a slower, gentler way to reconnect with life.

This chapter invites you to reflect, not diagnose. If you're unsure whether you're feeling bored or depressed, ask yourself:

- Do I feel curious, even a little?
- Can I observe my thoughts without drowning in them?
- Is there a part of me that wants to understand what's happening inside?

f the answer to any of these is yes, you're likely in boredom's landscape—not depression's. But if everything feels heavy, numb, or hopeless, that's when Boredomism steps back and makes room for real emotional care. Because stillness should feel like a return to self, not an exile from it.

Remember, boredom is not dangerous. What makes it uncomfortable is that it strips away the distractions that keep our pain at bay. That's not failure. That's honesty. And if you stay long enough in that space, even with the discomfort, something new begins to form—not as joy, not as clarity, but simply as presence.

You don't need to fix boredom. You just need to trust that it's not an enemy. When given space and time, boredom becomes the bridge between numbness and awareness, between burnout and breath, between avoidance and awakening. And in that quiet, you may discover not depression—but the slow reawakening of your own attention.

CHAPTER TWENTY

THE THRESHOLD OF ESCAPE

There is a moment—quiet, tense, and deeply uncomfortable—that almost everyone reaches when they begin to sit with boredom. It's the moment where the silence gets too loud. The stillness starts to feel unbearable. You may fidget, reach for your phone, suddenly remember a task that "must" be done, or feel an invisible itch that urges you to move. This is what Boredomism calls the threshold of escape—the precise edge where boredom threatens to become something deeper.

It's a psychological cliff. One that reveals how much of our daily motion is not chosen, but reactive. And the most important thing to know is this: crossing that threshold is not a sign of failure—it is a sign of arrival. You are arriving at the unfiltered experience of yourself, and for most people, that is unfamiliar territory.

Escaping isn't always dramatic. Often, it's subtle. It's the sudden urge to check a message. To reorganize something that doesn't need organizing. To open a browser "just for a second." To plan something. To eat. These aren't bad impulses—but they reveal something: the discomfort of presence. The fear of the void. Not a physical emptiness, but a mental and emotional stillness that we've been trained to avoid.

Why is it so hard to stay? Because on the other side of this silence lies everything we've buried. Restlessness is a symptom of internal resistance—not to boredom, but to what boredom might uncover. It may be unresolved emotions. Unfelt grief. Unmet needs. Forgotten memories. Quiet longings. Truths we've numbed through action.

The threshold of escape isn't just a moment—it's a mirror. It reflects our relationship with the uncomfortable parts of our being. And because modern life has taught us to equate stimulation with safety, we confuse stillness with threat. But Boredomism invites a reversal: what if stimulation is the escape, and stillness is the return?

In that moment—when you want to reach, scroll, move, distract—you are being offered something rare. A chance to stay. A chance to be with yourself in a state that does not demand performance, progress, or polish. This is where healing begins, not because we fix anything, but because we stop running.

Crossing the threshold doesn't mean you won't feel uncomfortable. In fact, you probably will. Your mind might scream that you're wasting time. That you're being irresponsible. That this doesn't matter. And yet—something quieter begins to rise beneath that noise. The voice you've been trying to hear. The clarity you've been chasing. The still awareness that has always been there, patiently waiting for you to pause long enough to listen.

Staying beyond the threshold does not require strength. It requires permission—permission to be with yourself without needing to be elsewhere. Without needing to justify your presence through action. You don't have to do anything. You don't have to earn this stillness. It is already yours.

This chapter is not a challenge. It's a reminder. The urge to escape is normal. It means your mind is conditioned to move. But every time you sit through that moment without reacting, you deepen your capacity for presence. You build a kind of inner muscle—not one that controls, but one that trusts.

And slowly, the threshold becomes familiar. The itch becomes quieter. The need to escape loses its urgency. What once felt unbearable begins to feel like a doorway. A slow, sacred threshold not into discomfort, but into depth.

Silence as a Philosophy of Return

We began this journey by questioning boredom—by wondering if, perhaps, it wasn't a flaw, but a forgotten doorway. Along the way, we slowed down. We sat still. We resisted escape. And somewhere in that process, we began to remember. Not just what it means to rest, but what it means to exist without expectation. Now, at the edge of this philosophy, we do not stand at a conclusion. We stand at a quiet beginning. This final part of the book is not about closure. It's about return.

Silence, in Boredomism, is not simply the absence of noise. It is a space where the self becomes visible again—where the distractions have settled, and what remains is what was always true. We are not returning to a version of ourselves we've never known; we are returning to a self that existed before the world told us to always become something more. Here, in the philosophy of return, we stop seeking answers and start listening to what remains when there are no more questions.

This is not a dramatic awakening. There are no firework insights. No "aha" moments. Just subtle shifts. A change in how we meet the day. A softening in how we speak to ourselves. A slowness in how we move through life. And though these shifts may seem small, they are not insignificant. They are the difference between living and rushing, between existing and constantly proving that existence.

In this final part, we no longer resist boredom. We no longer attempt to conquer it or explain it. We let it live with us. We let it become part of our rhythm. It is no longer a space we must endure, but a state we can trust. A place where insight blooms not from thought, but from presence. And in this presence, the need to be extraordinary falls away. What's left is not perfection. It's peace.

You may find that some of the urgency you once carried is already gone. Not because life slowed down, but because you did. And with that slowing, something else has returned—your breath, your awareness, your time. You have reclaimed them not through discipline, but through stillness. And that stillness now forms the foundation of your presence.

This part of the book does not aim to teach. It does not ask for effort. It offers only reflections. Meditations. Open-ended thoughts. They are not here to be solved, but to be sat with. They will ask you to be with yourself in a way you may have avoided. And they will suggest—gently, without pressure—that silence might not just be something to endure, but something to live in.

If the earlier chapters were about understanding and practicing Boredomism, these final pages are about embodying it. Let them meet you slowly. Let them be unfinished. Let them remain open. Because you are unfinished. And in that incompletion, there is beauty.

This is not the end of Boredomism. This is where it begins to live in you.

CHAPTER TWENTY-ONE

SUBTLE SHIFTS

Transformation is not always a loud affair. Sometimes, it doesn't look like change at all—not from the outside. There is no applause, no breakthrough moment, no grand unveiling. But inside, something has realigned. This is the nature of boredomism's effect: its power lies in the subtle shifts that quietly reshape the way we exist, without demanding attention or reward.

When you first begin the practice of boredom—not escaping it, not resisting it—you may not notice much. At best, it feels calm. At worst, mildly frustrating. But over time, without trying, you begin to see the world differently. Not in bold strokes, but in details: you find yourself pausing between tasks instead of rushing to the next one. You feel less guilty about a day "wasted." You begin to notice light, shadow, texture. You begin to see again, not just look. These are not just new habits. These are new patterns of being.

The world doesn't slow down, but you do. You walk without headphones. You sip something slowly. You sit in a café without pretending to be busy. And in these spaces, something long forgotten starts to return: a sense of being enough, just as you are. That's the core shift. Not that life becomes easier, or less demanding—but that your relationship to motion, urgency, and achievement begins to loosen.

You may also begin to notice your responses to discomfort changing. Where once you would reach for your phone, now you pause. Where you would once numb yourself with distraction, now you sit, even for a moment, and feel. This is not perfection—it's presence. And presence, over time, becomes your baseline, not your reward. It's not something you earn at the end of a long week. It's something you return to throughout the day.

What boredomism teaches you is that not everything has to be meaningful to matter. A silent afternoon. A slow cup of tea. A thought that drifts in and drifts out. These aren't trivial—they are anchors. They ground you in the kind of life that is not chasing purpose, but living from it. That's a deep shift: from seeking life to participating in it.

Another subtle but profound change happens in the way you value time. You may no longer feel the need to "spend" time efficiently. Instead, time becomes space. A place to be in, rather than something to get through. This shift changes how you relate to work, to rest, to your own inner life. Boredom becomes less of a block and more of a bridge—an entry point into your inner landscape.

Perhaps the most surprising shift, though, is emotional. With less noise in your mind, feelings that once overwhelmed you begin to soften. You find more clarity between reaction and response. You stop needing to explain every mood, fix every feeling, solve every moment. You begin to trust that just being with your experience, without control, is enough to allow it to pass through you.

These shifts are hard to measure, but they are unmistakable. A person who has embraced boredomism may still live in the same world, work the same job, carry the same responsibilities—but their way of being is different. They move through the day less hurried. They carry their presence like an inner still lake. They are less compelled to prove themselves, less caught in the web of urgency, more open to what unfolds naturally.

And this change—the quiet one, the one that no one claps for—is the deepest change of all. It doesn't look like success, but it feels like peace. It feels like coming home to something you forgot you had. It feels like your life is no longer happening in front of you, but through you. Slowly, and softly, boredomism brings you back to yourself.

65

CHAPTER TWENTY-TWO

TOWARD A SLOW FUTURE

We often think of the future in terms of acceleration—faster technology, faster communication, faster results. Progress has become synonymous with speed, and anything that slows us down is seen as backward or inefficient. But Boredomism proposes a radical alternative: what if the future worth imagining isn't faster, but slower? What if we are not meant to outrun time, but to return to its natural rhythm?

A slow future doesn't mean stagnation. It means depth over acceleration. It means reorienting our lives around what matters, rather than what's urgent. It means creating systems, routines, and cultures that allow for reflection, presence, and rest. In the philosophy of Boredomism, this isn't laziness—it's evolution. A society that doesn't know how to be still is a society constantly burning itself out.

We are witnessing the cracks already: chronic anxiety, emotional fatigue, shallow attention, and the growing inability to sit with silence. The current pace is unsustainable. People are producing more, but feeling less. Consuming more, but understanding less. Sharing more, but connecting less. We've been sprinting for decades—and now, many of us are out of breath.

The slow future Boredomism envisions is not about returning to the past. It's not a rejection of technology or progress. It's a recalibration. A conscious shift toward intentional engagement rather than compulsive reaction. Imagine digital spaces that reward depth instead of immediacy. Work cultures that honor rest as part of productivity. Education systems that allow space for boredom, creativity, and independent thought. Relationships that unfold, instead of being constantly maintained.

Slowness is not a limitation—it's a space for depth. Consider the natural world: trees grow slowly. Rivers carve valleys over centuries. Stars take millions of years to form and die. Nothing meaningful in nature happens in haste. Humans, too, were designed to move with rhythm—not in frantic loops, but in cycles of activity and restoration. To live in slowness is not to resist the future, but to move with it more wisely.

This future is not just philosophical—it's practical. A slow future would value fewer but deeper conversations. Fewer tasks with more meaning. Less distraction, more attention. Less content, more context. It invites us to redesign not only how we work and live, but how we define a life well-lived. The metrics would shift from "how much" to "how well." From "how fast" to "how fully."

There's also a spiritual tone to this vision. Not necessarily religious, but reverent. In a slow future, time is not seen as a threat but as a companion. Boredom is not feared but understood. The unknown is not avoided but sat with. Stillness becomes a societal skill—not just a personal one. And as individuals become more present, the collective begins to reflect that same presence.

But here's the most important truth: the slow future doesn't begin with policy or systems. It begins with you. With each moment you resist the urge to rush. Each time you choose stillness over noise. Each time you sit without a purpose and find yourself more alive, not less. These small acts are not insignificant. They are seeds of cultural change.

Boredomism does not seek to escape the world. It seeks to deepen it. A slow future doesn't mean stepping backward—it means stepping inward. Into a world where the soul is no longer outpaced by the schedule. Into a life where attention is sacred, silence is nourishing, and time is no longer our enemy.

This is not a utopian dream. It is a conscious choice. A daily rebellion against the fast, and a daily return to what is full, even when it appears empty. The future, if we are wise, will not be a blur. It will be a breath. And in that breath, we will remember what it feels like to be human again.

CHAPTER TWENTY-THREE

Unmeasured Living

We are born into a world of measurements. From our first moments, we're weighed, scored, compared. School grades follow. Test results. Salaries. Followers. Achievements. Even our rest must now be tracked: sleep apps, step counters, productivity journals. This system trains us, quietly but powerfully, to believe that what cannot be measured doesn't matter.

But what if the most meaningful parts of life—presence, joy, clarity, quiet—cannot be quantified at all?

Unmeasured living is Boredomism's answer to the tyranny of metrics. It is the practice of releasing yourself from the grip of constant self-evaluation. It means experiencing life without reducing it to units of usefulness or data points of growth. It doesn't reject structure or reflection—it simply refuses to live under their rule.

We are not inherently obsessed with measurement. It's a habit. One inherited, taught, reinforced. In a society shaped by capitalism, worth is often tied to output: what you earn, what you produce, how fast you progress. This mindset doesn't just affect work—it bleeds into creativity, relationships, even self-worth. We begin to believe that unless something can be shown, posted, proved, or tracked—it lacks value. And that belief slowly steals our ability to feel fulfilled.

Boredomism invites you to see the absurdity of this. A walk in silence has value, even if you never count the steps. A day spent doing nothing has meaning, even if it doesn't produce anything. An afternoon of staring at clouds is not wasted—it is lived. The beauty of life isn't always seen when we look harder. Sometimes, it emerges only when we stop trying to grasp it.

When you live unmeasured, time becomes elastic again. You stop slicing it into segments of productivity. A moment of stillness can feel like an hour of depth. You're no longer racing to meet imaginary timelines or life milestones. You begin to trust your internal rhythms, not the ones imposed by culture, algorithms, or planners.

Of course, this isn't always easy. The mind, shaped by years of comparison, will resist. It will whisper: "You're falling behind." "You didn't do enough today." "Prove you're improving." These voices don't disappear overnight. But unmeasured living doesn't fight them—it sees them, smiles gently, and doesn't obey.

This way of living is not about becoming indifferent. It's about becoming aware. Aware of when measurement begins to dominate your sense of self. Aware of when you are turning your inner world into a scoreboard. In those moments, Boredomism suggests not a strategy, but a pause. Step back. Breathe. And remember: you are not your metrics.

Imagine living one day where nothing you did was judged, recorded, or compared. Not even by you. You simply existed. You moved slowly. You responded honestly. You were present not to optimize the moment, but to feel it. That is what unmeasured living looks like. And in that day, you may find more clarity than a hundred pages of planning ever gave you.

This chapter is a gentle rebellion. Not against structure—but against enslavement to it. It is a permission slip to live a little looser. To trust your sense of enoughness without needing to prove it.

Because in the end, no one will remember how much you tracked. They will remember how fully you lived. And you will remember how it felt to finally be free—not from responsibility, but from the quiet pressure to constantly become. In that freedom, you will find not emptiness—but a kind of richness that can never be counted.

71

CHAPTER TWENTY-FOUR

The Philosophy of Absence

What if meaning didn't always come from what is present—but from what is missing? What if absence, often treated as a void or a lack, was actually one of the richest forms of presence we can experience? The Philosophy of Absence is a key pillar in Boredomism's quiet architecture. It is a way of seeing emptiness not as failure, but as fertility. Not as silence, but as a space where truth has room to echo.

Our culture fears absence. We fill every gap, every pause, every blank space with something—noise, content, commentary, consumption. We have been conditioned to believe that value only arises when something is added. That meaning must be made visible, loud, and measurable. But Boredomism asks: what if we've misunderstood emptiness altogether?

Absence isn't just the space between things—it is the condition that allows things to exist meaningfully at all. Imagine music without silence. Imagine language without pauses. Imagine life without rest. The spaces in between are not interruptions—they are structure. Without them, everything collapses into chaos, noise, and burnout.

In personal experience, absence often arrives in moments we call "boredom." These are the stretches of time where there is no agenda, no stimulation, and no defined purpose. And yet, these moments are not empty. They are alive with potential. It is in those blank spaces that your mind reorganizes itself, your emotions settle, and something real begins to surface—not because you chased it, but because you stopped long enough to let it appear.

The Philosophy of Absence teaches us to value what is not there. The unsent message. The unspoken word. The decision not to act. The time left unfilled. These moments, often invisible from the outside, carry immense internal weight. They restore balance. They create boundaries. They invite reflection. And they remind us that we don't need to constantly fill to feel whole.

Absence also gives birth to contemplation, the very heartbeat of philosophical inquiry. When we are constantly stimulated, we react. But when we sit in the gap—without distraction—we begin to see. Our inner world, often drowned in noise, begins to rise. We see patterns. We recognize illusions. We rediscover emotions long buried. Absence, then, becomes a tool of awareness. A way to remember what's underneath.

To live with the Philosophy of Absence is not to withdraw from life—it is to re-enter life with intention. It is to choose not to speak when silence says more. It is to cancel the extra meeting not because you're lazy, but because you've learned that space is sacred. It is to resist the pressure to explain yourself, post online, react instantly, or fill every evening with activity. Not as avoidance, but as alignment.

Some may misunderstand this approach as apathy. But there is a quiet distinction between disengagement and discernment. Absence, in the context of Boredomism, is not disconnection from meaning—it is a return to it. By stepping away from the noise, we give our attention back its weight. We allow life to unfold at its own rhythm.

And in time, we stop being afraid of gaps. We welcome them. We create them. We need them. Because we know what they offer: stillness, insight, recovery, honesty, and breath. The world will always tempt us to fill—but we now understand that sometimes, the most meaningful thing you can add is nothing at all.

CHAPTER TWENTY-FIVE

BOREDOMISM IN CONVERSATION WITH MODERN PHILOSOPHIES

I. The Value of Philosophical Dialogue

No philosophy stands completely alone—not even the most original ones. Every meaningful system of thought grows in response to questions that have echoed for centuries. Boredomism emerges not as a disruption of philosophical history, but as a continuation of it—a modern answer to a very old human tension: how do we live with presence in a world built for distraction?

This chapter explores how Boredomism enters into thoughtful dialogue with other major philosophical traditions—not to imitate, but to interact. Through these comparisons, we don't weaken Boredomism's originality—we strengthen its roots.

II. Stoicism – Controlling the Reaction vs. Sitting With It

Stoicism teaches that we cannot control what happens to us, only how we respond. Its core is the development of inner composure through self-regulation and rational detachment. Boredomism shares Stoicism's calm demeanor, but diverges in its emotional posture.

Where Stoicism aims to master emotion, Boredomism allows it. Stoics discipline the reaction; boredomists sit beside it. In the stillness of boredom, we don't always analyze our emotional discomfort—we observe it, softly, without trying to improve or defeat it.

Both philosophies promote non-reactivity—but Stoicism values virtue through discipline, while Boredomism values clarity through surrender. They complement each other, but their methods differ.

III. Existentialism – From Meaninglessness to Presence

Existentialist thinkers—like Kierkegaard, Sartre, and Camus—addressed the human confrontation with meaninglessness. Boredom, to them, often appeared as a symptom of existential crisis: an inner awareness that life may not contain inherent purpose. Kierkegaard called boredom "the root of all evil," and Camus saw it in the monotony of daily life.

Boredomism meets these same themes but changes the posture. Instead of demanding meaning, it suggests we rest inside the question. Where existentialists often leaned into rebellion, Boredomism leans into presence. The moment does not need to be profound to be worthy of attention.

Existentialism asks: What is the purpose of all this?
Boredomism replies: What if we sit with that question, without answering?

IV. Absurdism – A Shared Tolerance for Silence

Absurdism, especially in Camus' vision, explores the conflict between our desire for meaning and the indifference of the universe. Boredom is often a byproduct of this contradiction—a mental pause where neither the world nor the self delivers an answer.

Where Camus proposes defiance (imagine Sisyphus happy), Boredomism proposes stillness. Instead of pushing the boulder again, perhaps Sisyphus can sit for a while. Not to quit life, but to see what arises when we stop performing. Not everything must be resisted. Some absurdities can be absorbed.

In this way, Boredomism does not deny absurdity—it rests with it, until the edges soften and something wordless begins to feel real again.

V. Phenomenology – First-Person Awareness and Still Perception

Phenomenology, as developed by Husserl and Heidegger, studies conscious experience from the inside out. It asks not just what things are, but how they appear to us. Boredomism works within this same field: it prioritizes the direct, lived moment—before interpretation, before productivity, before judgment.

In Boredomism, when we sit still, we encounter the world with fresh eyes. A wall, a breath, a breeze—none of these are remarkable. But all of them, when truly perceived, become profound in their ordinariness. Like phenomenology, Boredomism is not interested in theories about life—it's interested in how life feels when you stop editing it.

To do nothing, and to attend to that nothing, is a phenomenological act of reclaiming consciousness.

VI. American Pragmatism – The Usefulness of "Useless" Experience

William James and the American Pragmatists placed great value on experience over abstraction. Truth, they argued, is what works for us—what lives well in the real world. Boredomism shares this grounding. It is not a lofty ideal. It is something you feel, live, and return to when you've exhausted life's overstimulated rhythms.

Boredom may not seem "useful" in the pragmatic sense, but its usefulness is paradoxical. It allows emotional rest, mental integration, and creative space. The silence it brings has no outcome—but the outcome is often clarity. James might not have called it productive, but he might have recognized its quiet efficacy.

Boredomism doesn't try to prove itself philosophically—it invites you to try it, and see what changes.

VII. Critical Theory – The Rebellion Against Productive Time

The Frankfurt School thinkers—Adorno, Horkheimer, Marcuse—critiqued how capitalist systems colonize time and consciousness. Under such systems, even rest is monetized, even thought is made efficient. Leisure becomes guilt. Slowness becomes sin.

Boredomism enters this space as a philosophical resistance. It suggests that doing nothing is not laziness but liberation. It rejects internalized productivity as the measure of worth. To sit still, without trying to optimize yourself, is not only healthy—it is radical.

Boredomism allows time to return to the individual. Not clock time. Not market time. But human time—unmeasured, uneven, and deeply alive.

VIII. Minimalism – Space for What Truly Matters

Modern Minimalism teaches the removal of excess, the stripping down of life to essentials. Boredomism resonates here but adds an internal layer. Minimalism removes visual clutter. Boredomism removes cognitive and emotional clutter.

It asks: once you've simplified your space, can you sit quietly within it? Can you live in the pause, not just create it? Boredomism doesn't just make room—it teaches you how to be in the room, without reaching for the next distraction.

IX. Modern Mindfulness – Awareness Without Utility

Contemporary mindfulness practices encourage attention to breath, thought, and body. But in many cases, even mindfulness becomes another task—something to do, to complete, to perfect.

Boredomism steps gently away from this. It welcomes attention, but not as a goal. You don't sit to feel better, breathe better, or live longer. You sit because there is nowhere else you need to be. It is not structured, not guided, not optimized. It is a simple presence.

Boredomism strips away the intention to improve. And in doing so, reveals a state of being that asks for nothing, but gives quietly in return.

X. A Philosophy in Its Own Right

Boredomism doesn't require the authority of past traditions to be valid. But these comparisons reveal its depth. It listens to the ideas of those who came before it—and then, it sits in silence and asks: What do I feel now? What remains when there is nothing left to chase?

In this stillness, it earns its place.

CHAPTER TWENTY-SIX

A QUIET GOODBYE

There is a tendency, even in books like this, to end with something grand. A call to action. A final summary. A motivational sendoff. But Boredomism does not believe in crescendos. It does not believe in climax. It believes in the slow, the quiet, the unfinished. So, this chapter will not offer closure in the way you might expect. Instead, it offers a kind of disappearance. A gentle fade, like the hush of the world just before sleep.

A philosophy built around stillness should not end with a bang—it should dissolve, like mist. If you've come this far, it means you've sat with ideas, feelings, and maybe even discomfort that many avoid. You've not only read about boredom—you've considered it, maybe even practiced it. And that alone means something has shifted.

But Boredomism isn't something you "complete." You don't graduate from it. You don't master it. You simply begin to carry it with you, quietly. Not as a set of rules, but as a rhythm. It becomes a presence—something that hums beneath the busyness of your days, reminding you that you can stop. That you are allowed to pause. That you don't need to chase meaning for it to arise.

You may forget this philosophy sometimes. That's okay. You may find yourself swept back into the noise, into the constant scroll, the rush, the restlessness. That's okay too. Boredomism doesn't demand perfection. It isn't a lifestyle to uphold—it's a home to return to. Again and again. When you're tired. When you're lost.

When you feel the weight of doing pressing down too heavily. The invitation will still be there: Do nothing. Just be here.

Perhaps the greatest gift of Boredomism is not what it adds to your life, but what it removes. The pressure to perform. The expectation to produce. The guilt of resting. The fear of missing out. It slowly unravels the internal dialogue that tells you your worth is somewhere outside of you, waiting to be earned. In its place, it leaves a silence. Not empty—but alive.

This quiet goodbye is not a conclusion. It is a continuation. The book may end, but the practice doesn't. You may never need to return to these pages again, or you might come back often. Either way, the real philosophy now lives not in this text—but in the spaces between your actions. In the pauses. In the gaps. In the stillness that you begin to choose instead of fear.

And if, someday, you find yourself sitting on a bench, or lying on the floor, or staring at the ceiling with nothing to do—nothing to chase, fix, or finish—you'll know: this is it. This is the practice. This is the path. This is enough.

So, we end not with a lesson, but with a permission:
You may now leave. You may now stay. You may now do nothing at all.

This, after all, is the art.

Afterword

There is no true ending to a philosophy built on stillness.
There are only pauses — spaces between moments, where awareness breathes and the self softens.

As you close this book, you are not asked to remember everything you have read. You are not asked to adopt new rules or chase new ideals.

You are invited simply to live — slowly, attentively, quietly — in a way that feels more like a return than an arrival.

Stillness is not a place to reach. It is where you already are, beneath the motion and the noise.

If Boredomism has offered you even a small glimpse of that truth, then it has fulfilled its purpose.

The journey continues, but not in haste. It continues, in you, wherever you pause long enough to notice.

A Note To The Reader

Thank you for walking through these pages with me.

You could have been anywhere else — rushing, scrolling, chasing — and yet you chose to pause here, in this quiet space. That choice matters.

Remember: doing nothing is not wasting time.

It is meeting time.

It is meeting yourself.

May you carry this philosophy with you, not as a burden, but as a lightness you can return to — whenever you forget that you are already enough.